Here Comes the Parade

Written by Clare Mishica   **Illustrated by Ilene Richard**

Children's Press®
A Division of Scholastic Inc.
New York • Toronto • London • Auckland • Sydney
Mexico City • New Delhi • Hong Kong
Danbury, Connecticut

For Syd and Christian, who like to celebrate life.
— C.M.

To Mom and Dad, my biggest supporters.
— I.R.

Consultant
Eileen Robinson
Reading Specialist

Library of Congress Cataloging-in-Publication Data

Mishica, Clare, 1960–
    Here comes the parade / written by Clare Mishica ;
illustrated by Ilene Richard.
        p. cm. — (A Rookie reader)
    Summary: Clowns, marching bands, and other participants in a lively parade
introduce the numbers from one to ten.
    ISBN 0-516-24857-X (lib. bdg.)   0-516-25016-7 (pbk.)
    [1. Parades—Fiction. 2. Counting.] I. Richard, Ilene, ill. II. Title. III. Series.
    PZ7.M6843He 2005
    [E]—dc22
                                2004030157

CHILDREN'S PRESS and A ROOKIE READER®, and associated logos are trademarks
and or registered trademarks of Scholastic Library Publishing. SCHOLASTIC and
associated logos are trademarks and or registered trademarks of Scholastic Inc.
1 2 3 4 5 6 7 8 9 10 R 14 13 12 11 10 09 08 07 06 05

Here comes the parade!

I see one police car.

Two marching bands.

Three horses.

Four bicycles.

Five drums.

Six dogs.

15

Seven clowns.

17

Eight motorcycles.

Nine flags.

Ten balloons.

But there are too many people to count!

Word List (36 Words)

(Words in **bold** help readers count.)

are	dogs	marching	**ten**
balloons	drums	motorcycles	the
bands	**eight**	**nine**	there
bicycles	**five**	**one**	**three**
but	flags	parade	to
car	**four**	people	too
clowns	here	police	**two**
comes	horses	see	
count	I	**seven**	
	many	**six**	

About the Author

Clare Mishica lives on the Keweenaw Peninsula in Upper Michigan. In the winter, there's lots of snow for skiing and sledding, and in the summer, Lake Superior offers both sand and pebble beaches to explore. She enjoys writing children's stories, painting, making stained glass art, reading, and spending time with her family and friends.

About the Illustrator

Ilene Richard was a successful jewelry designer before getting back to illustrating children's books. She has illustrated many books in both the trade and educational markets. Ilene lives with her husband Lawrence, her daughter Jodi, her son Corey, and their dog Bess in Andover, Massachusetts.